BEING

PATRICIA HELEN WOOLDRIDGE

Cinnamon Press
:: small miracles from distinctive voices ::

Published by Cinnamon Press
www.cinnamonpress.com
Office 49019, PO Box 92, Cardiff, CF11 1NB

The right of Patricia Helen Wooldridge to be identified as author of this work has been asserted by her in accordance with the Copyright, Designs and Patent Act, 1988. Copyright © 2021 Patricia Helen Wooldridge ISBN: 978-1-78864-075-6
British Library Cataloguing in Publication Data. A CIP record for this book can be obtained from the British Library.

Designed and typeset in Palatino by Cinnamon Press.
Cover design by Adam Craig.
Cinnamon Press is represented in the UK by Inpress Ltd and in Wales by the Books Council of Wales.

Acknowledgements

I wish to thank the editors of the following publications where some of these poems have appeared occasionally in slightly different versions: 'Snow Moon' was published in *Trio & Other Poets*, Cinnamon Press, 2015; 'In the Belly of the Woods', 'Woodland Tilt' and 'There was talk of summer…' were published in *From Hallows to Harvest*, ed. Adam Craig, Cinnamon Press, 2019; 'Heron' was a prizewinner for 'Poems on the Buses', Guernsey International Poetry Competition 2020 (judged by Simon Armitage); 'Opposing Directions' was published in *Obsessed with Pipework*, no. 18, 2002; Part of 'Sea Fret' first appeared as 'Pink Coat' published in *Iota*, no. 76, 2007.

The references to Heraclitus (in 'Heraclitus at Aldeburgh') are taken from the Penguin Classics edition, translated by Brooks Haxton, 2001.

Contents

Being

for Nick, with love

Snow Moon

Lounging across the clawed

bark of a mountain ash,

a snowball moon melts

from its low slung branches,

lopes out onto frosted snow,

wide eye scanning the dark,

a lean on night's scent.

Stare into its open mouth

its pocked face…

Invisible

Old snow across a garden
sodden in last year.

In the open field
a horse has nowhere else to go,

her drooping head
in the north-westerly,

bound in one strip
of electric wire

with no dry place.
I am not myself;

a few loose catkins
drooping lines,

sifting words
I couldn't live without—

love, sky, blue…

where one white horse
tastes the wind,

another razed on chalk,
forever strolling—

I cling to this rasping pencil voice.

Naming

For the first time in over a week, the sun appears.

Walk in the forest, dry underfoot—a red admiral
flutters then basks on the sand in front

this first Christmas since my mother died.

The red-orange ball slips behind trees
where there is a gap in the downs to catch its fall.

Find the moon by climbing to the highest bridge—
two days old, Venus in its sling.

No break in overcast cold. Yesterday redwings
on the field muttering like starlings only lighter.

Fieldfares and a mistle thrush calling. Several mice
in a stand of holly in the middle of a ploughed field.

I have a mid-winter dream—a ship on a frozen river—
my mother's voice… my name, my name.

I write, therefore…

Out early, the river slick black, sugary snow
in heaps on the holly, flung over bracken.

The palette cinnamon and white. Love these
first silhouettes, standing in the edge,

crow cawing, jay on alarm, buttery light.
A hint of tan in the oaks' holding leaf.

Walk north to a sixth sense in the field —
there at the sides of my eyes —

a shadow going east, going west.

I leave a trace on every fence and stile,
not a bird in sound except a robin's threads.

Arrive at the bridge to a full assembly
of crows, jackdaws, rooks — inky drops

on poplar spires and my finger scores:
I am

Song

even in snow
a bullfinch sings
the long held oak leaves fall

Today the thickest rime I have ever seen.

Travelling through overhung branches,
tiny spears packed on every edge

for they have bathed in snow-breath.

A goldcrest close up in the woods,
nuthatch emits his machine-gun trill.

Lost in all this weather,
a blackbird finds his song.

Interlude (1)

Sky the colour of gulls

on this chilled one degree day

waiting for a sign —

a rill of snow on the car but nothing comes of it

sparrows have their cluster chat

two egrets a surprise on the lake —

heron taking off, folding the air

a fine shaking out settles on my sleeve,

then a flurry for half an hour —

afternoon mizzles out to a snow blush…

In the Belly of the Woods

The river's full

   and a pliable brown

siskins   wittering   high in the alders

almost in the water   hanging loose

   a clump of snowdrops

to stroll among thousands

   woodland veins on cold breath sky

where the snowdrops have it

   in satin   three petals wide

sprung   in a glance of sun.

February…

sneaking out of winter,
rare day of blue haze, bright if raw,

ground frost embittered,
spawning fog with the dawn,

it could be snowing or not…

Two hours walking, diaphanous clouds,
fall in beside these snowdrop clusters,

sit beside them barely lilting
on the anniversary of my mother's death—

a wooded bank in wild daffodils,
one blackthorn early in the lane—

discover a hint of marzipan,
a bumble bee drooping blooms

before imminent rain,
drenching, non-stop deliverance.

Meeting

Dunnocks ringing out with great tits' variations.
Love seeing sheep back on the field—much sitting down.
Already in a day track lines visible.

Down to the stream and the rooks are active,
sticks drop as I pass. A mistle thrush towards Steep Marsh,
on to the horse field—so pleased I did—

redwings chittering as they pick over dung.
Green woodpecker yaffling, jays on alarm
stop by the river, check for mandarins

but only mallards paddling in the shallows—
raise binoculars—I'm looking at a wet roe deer
standing in the middle of the flow staring back at me.

We hold our gaze—those large ears and eyes,
then she continues to nibble at the water weed
at 8.00 am, unbothered until a car arrives—

that splash and straddled lunge, melting into dry woods.

Interlude (2)

A lantern sun on pause

    like crepe paper in tangerine—

sparrows lively, blackbird sings each morning

    frog spawn arrived three days ago

never mind the flurries

    in the leaf litter bluebell shoots.

Clouds watery blue, two deer grazing,

    frozen pond by the fishery

a pair of mallards perch

    on an overhanging branch asleep,

something—coming round river—

    grey wagtail like a moth in misted dawn.

When the sun emerges there is a lightness of self.

A Hampshire Greeting

Them badgers've gone quiet —
the old man stops and says,

nodding over where I'm watching
blades sluicing into muck.

Three bluebells, a stitchwort,
sprig of cow parsley

droop in my hand, while
we listen to the plough.

Drawing me back to a scar
in the bank, he lifts a hair from the wire,

rolls it over the back of his hand —
a badger hair bumps, that's how you tell,

sometimes see their prints across the lane —
a little bit of England...

Woodland Tilt

Climb into hanging woods
lean   over   the canopy

summer is a glass of water
showing nothing but a silver skin

remember the small but magnificent waterfall
in midwinter crescendo—

please   keep on falling

by July think only   hydrangea
bubbling cumulus   flirting with land

> *tonight the stars*
> *with only time for three*
> *on a velvet dusk*

> *the swifts continue*
> *tearing the others away*

There was talk of summer…

what should have been a glut
of raspberries   bleeds

rain-lashed trees   hydra heads
swimming in a green tide
potatoes   too sodden to lift

I rinse out my pen
note   plump sloes in July
the colour of ink

begin as if there were
no beginning   August deleted

when I hear the laugh that comes
for no other reason than

three morning glories are open.

Heron

Can't believe the heron landing on our house

long arrow beak and doubling height
    of his unfurled neck

bones opening in my spine

or last night the ash a scaffold for the moon —

snowball caught in a web

or this morning spider lines guyed to the tree

hanging out to weigh a soggy sun

or the heron's pendulous flop on a too-small-tree

a would-be-snake sun-streaked

reaching until

we're both swallowing the blunt ends of summer.

Interlude (3)

October is a surprise...

    muzzling the air

where one warm day

    hovers on a festival of bloom

Michaelmas daisies

    silky as a spaniel's ears

first fieldfares

    across my walk

a trail of mist

    spinning from self

        pulling from my core.

Opposing Directions

Tonight clouds ruck
in opposing directions,
the slip-stream glows yellow-white
like the coolest flame;

a grey tube unrolls
below sliding sands,
smokes out the light until a blue-white
glaze holds the evening in a fug.

Broken strata, mackerel scales
and a flare of horse tails,

one burnt ochre rim;
blind spots on the page
furred round the edge
like oil on the road after rain.

Where the water lies…

The familiars of November
        pucker through these tonal greys,
our wintering birds are back
        and smoke churns the clear days.

A call to light, nestling water
        bedding in this suddenness
of turned earth, flustered leaves
        and gathering Brent geese.

In the crimping silver glaze,
        puddled land shrinks to a line
of muddy green and the sun sinks
        into haze low across the brine

of salt-marsh, a charcoal sketch
        to frame sky, scatter these flights—
guttural seams that clear their throats
        on distance—the brow of word heights…

        and the short-eared owl
        glides back and forth so close
        I see wings full of ochre

Sea Fret

scattered pines lean,
wet grass, whistling ducks,
my shadow half the field long

Chase the sea fret of the mind,
lose myself in treelines

the stance of the silver birch
now a sequin scattering of yellow

love November's dank
drizzling chill, leaves drooping…

A woman running in pink polyester
full of air, the same pink as sea thrift—

like the wet trunks of chestnuts
I wear olive-brown

a gull call far inland—

ask her if she runs along the shore
with no retrace

if she has a pebble in her coat
squat in its pocket of damp.

Interlude (4)

A planet so light

    it will float

        in water

with all the breath

    from its own plethora

        of moons

humming inside the rings

    of resonant

        voices

spewed to shimmer

    collide and scatter

        forever

circling in a flux of ice

    playing out

        its song.

Heraclitus at Aldeburgh

1   *Things keep their secrets*

The sea—loud at 5.00 am
      in a rushing windswept way,
      mottled cloud, the odd star,
soft deep monochrome.

6.00 am—a skin of light held out
      on water (the moon pulling away),
      gulls in a hubbub, hanging first calls
in a stutter, joust against chimneys.

8.00 am slick into wavelets, two swimmers
      enter November wash, silver
      broken foil from a hole in sky,
navy blue horizon, taupe reverie.

One swallow skims the marsh (so late)
      not all make the journey back.

2   *The sun is new*
     again, all day

Sea state choppy

turgid brown waves
slinking towards Thorpness

at the scallop shell

lean into its side,
wait…

blip of fire blinding to disc
coating steel in oil of sun

when the sea is this roused
I back up the shingle.

3   *The earth is melted*
     into the sea
     by that same reckoning
     whereby the sea
     sinks into the earth

Gabions of stones —

crevice opportunity
for sea spurge roots

last house perched
on sea writhing corner

worrying cliff now sand
breaks the sea into *ness*

where disintegration
equals broken

picking up pocketfuls

I am as I am not
and ever will be…

Eulogy

The clouds spoke this morning
when the sun slunk into wax

the night before
hazy stars

and the inconsolable woman
in another room.

Now this stealthy sunrise
woollen bands of scolding flush

a wrinkled sea undulates
the windows are so clean.

Being

a symphony
of silent breathing
frost rising

Though day is just breaking

I'll take your picture

to show how skin

lifts the shadows of dark

in earthy tones,

even if rain

lies close behind

threatening to slip its grey net—

though the day is just breaking

and I take your picture

it wouldn't be enough

to catch each pore that

breathes this light,

especially when the sun

opens like a window

and paints you there.